From Me to

My No-nonsense Journey into Motherhood

Marie Smith

Dedication ...

For all of you amazing parents!

Contents

Dedication … 2

Introduction 4

How I am going to structure my book.. 6

Let's start with a bit of background on me....................................... 7

Ok – so the bit where I (we) decided to take the plunge 8

Pregnant... 11

Pre-Baby.. 13

Pre-Birth Preparations 16

The Birth... 20

The Baby - Feeding & Adapting 29

Baby Groups 37

The Baby - Sleeping Routines.. 39

The Baby - Weaning... 42

Life Now... 45

Summary Paragraph Family 48

Introduction

Ok, so I certainly do not claim to be an expert in this field but having acquired two lovely stepsons, and having my own daughter in 2017, I felt if even one person could benefit from the contents of this book it would be worth writing!

What is my aim here?

Well, let's see…

There are so many parenting books out there, all of which have their own wonderful tips, and tricks (which is great).

The ones I came across seemed very regimented and precise (probably for very good reason as many of these books utilise tried and tested methods across many areas of parenthood). Some covered sleep routines; some covered feeding; some covered playtime and education; the list goes on…

As useful as all these books were, they rather intimidated me. I worried about whether I would be a failure if I did not do things the same way; but then there were so many, 'set ways', depending on the book I read.

One thing I struggled to find at the time was your average person's experience of motherhood; their worries and experiences, and their tips and tricks if they found any!

I could not deny it, the prospect of being a parent scared the living daylights out of me! Being a generally relaxed individual, I really did worry about whether I would be a good mum.

It was all very overwhelming.

My aim with this book is to give you a bit of insight into me and my personal journey into motherhood. I hope it provides some reassurance that there are no set rules! Afterall we would all be rather boring if we were raised the same way wouldn't we!?

Don't get me wrong, we all want the best for our brood, and to raise as well-rounded an individual as possible, but I guess my focus is more on me and what I went through in the hope that it helps someone else with their journey! It is easy to put all emphasis on the little bundle of joy you have just pushed out (one way or another), but sometimes it's easy to forget that **we** are still here and having to learn how to cope with this little human that solely relies on us day and night. Sometimes these amazing books don't quite prepare you for that!

Lastly, I do not want this book to feel like a huge commitment for you to read. It is not a 500-page novel, but hopefully it provides enough detail to give you some useful information and can be something you can pick up and refer to if needed; a friendly reminder that you are doing great, regardless of how you are doing it!

How I am going to structure my book

In essence, my book isn't just about relaying my feelings and experiences to you for the sake of it. I want to create a comfortable setting where you can learn about these experiences, and if there are some parts that you relate to yourselves, whether you are a new mum, pregnant or thinking about having a baby, you will be able to take something positive away with you.

Each section of this book will cover various areas of my baby journey; from deciding to try and make one; my pregnancy; post-baby, and all in-between! Once I reach a point of reflection, I will add a **summary paragraph** so that if any of you do relate to my feelings or worries in any way, I can hopefully provide some reassurance that I experienced them too, that you are not alone and that its okay to feel this way.

At the end of this book, I have collated all my, 'Summary paragraphs', together, as these can be read alongside my story, **or** on their own as a bit of a, 'pick-me-up'.

Feel free to head straight toward the back and read these first, but please do come back to the front to let me share my story with you.

Let's start with a bit of background on me

Having been to university where I studied Design, I had been lucky enough to get a job in the industry pretty much from the get-go. I can quite easily say I was very happy with my child-free life. No commitments, no obligations, and no ties!

I had never really had a huge interest in having children at all in my twenties, but I did always have a niggle in the back of my mind that I would feel it necessary to experience what we are on this planet to do (apparently)....

I was around 26 when me and my partner Pete got together. He had two lovely sons from his previous relationship and because of this, I had the joy of being eased into some form of motherhood on weekends; holidays; birthdays; Christmases etc. **Don't get me wrong,** I know now that this glimpse into motherhood was nowhere near what was to come when having my own, but it was fun, and I absolutely adored those boys (still do).

Ok – so the bit where I (we) decided to take the plunge

Pete and I had been fortunate enough to buy our first property together five years before we had our daughter. It was a 3-bed new-build in the perfect location as it was close to work and our parents. Although I have (and still do) always had a desire to travel and see as much of this world that we live in as possible, I have always been a home-bird, and did like having my folks nearby.

When we were getting things sorted and talking about how we would utilise the two back bedrooms, I knew that having a spare room was the right thing to do. The boys shared the bigger of the two rooms and the third, box room was turned into a dumping ground (I used to dread opening the door to it as there was so much crap crammed in there). In the back of my mind, I guess I always knew I needed this space reserved, you know, just in case!!

And this was how we rolled for a good few years or so. Work, life and trying to be grown-ups!

It was great!

On the weekends when we had the boys, we made plans to take them for days out and generally focused our attention on them and child-friendly activities. On the boy-free weekends we could revert to our lazy selves! We enjoyed late film nights in front of the TV with a takeaway, no set bedtime, and lie-ins the following morning!

I remember one New Year's Eve at a friend's house prior to me getting pregnant, she asked me when I would be having a child. I laughed it off and told her not to be daft. The conscious thought of having a baby had not entered my mind! Don't get me wrong, there was clearly a lot going on sub-consciously due to my allocation of the spare room, but I really hadn't visualised it happening any time soon.

I later mentioned it to Pete who also laughed but did not seem as scared of the prospect as I thought he would be! With him already having two, why would he want to go on this journey again!? Or at least that is what I had always told myself.

I think because of his laid-back reaction, having a baby now became more of a regular thought. I had suddenly become a person with a desire to have a child! I cannot say exactly when I became sure this was the direction I wanted to go in, but there it was...

... the need to have one!

I discussed this with Pete, and we went over how he felt about it. Although we had his two wonderful boys, he explained that he knew when we got together that having a child might be something I would want to do, so he had been okay about this for some time.

How cool is he!?

I was on the pill and had been for years so we agreed I would stop and just see how things went! I assumed that would be that, and we would be trying for a long time to conceive. **How wrong was I!**

Within less than a couple of months of stopping my pill, I had the suspicion I had missed a period. Now… using the word, 'suspicion', may seem odd, but a lot of my friends are as regular as clockwork and know exactly when they are due on within a day or so. Me on the other hand didn't have a clue. With being on the pill and not having any breaks (and therefore periods), to having periods again but being a bit too lazy to track them, I genuinely did not know whether I had really missed a period or not but felt it would be a good time to take a test just in case.

I picked up a cheap supermarket test for about a pound. I remember looking at the tests on the shelves and all the fancy extras you would get for spending an absolute fortune, but I figured a basic test would do pretty much the same thing! If I remember rightly, I did tell Pete I was thinking of doing one but didn't say exactly when that would be. We were both at home after a day at work and I decided to toddle off upstairs and take …

… the test!

Pregnant

So, there I was, sat on the loo with this test in my hand showing a positive result! I couldn't believe it! You would have thought I'd have been over the moon, after all I had been the one who had initiated all of this! But the feeling of fear, worry and uncertainty started to trickle in. I felt incredibly emotional and decided to go downstairs to discuss the news.

Pete was brilliant, he smiled straight away and said it was great! I sobbed and couldn't quite get my head around it. I was 30 and my whole life had pretty much been about me; I mean buying a house had been the most grown-up thing I had done until this point.

I booked a doctor's appointment where they tested me again and confirmed I was **STILL** pregnant. This then got the ball rolling with the letters requesting a booking-in appointment, first scan date and so on.

While I am on the topic of my booking-in appointment, I recall having this at the hospital and being asked the date I started my last period! Could I remember this? NOPE! I felt useless as I assume this was something you were supposed to know… whoops!

Summary Paragraph #1

When you find out you are pregnant, it is ok and perfectly normal to feel a bit odd about everything, even completely out of your depths. I couldn't really nail the exact emotion I felt when I found out; maybe it was a lot of varying emotions rolled into one!

It's also ok to question whether you have done the right thing, and it is ok to feel amazing and excited too!

At one point I did wonder whether I had made the right choice but looking back I can see it was a period of adjustment for me and coming to terms with the journey I was about to embark upon.

Looking back, I think I was very lucky that I managed to get caught pregnant so quickly. I have friends who tried for months and months before they managed to conceive. Whether it takes a few weeks or a few months, it is normally not anything to worry about and will hopefully happen in good time and when your body is ready.

Always trust your body and your feelings though, and if you have any concerns about conceiving do not hesitate to speak to a doctor about things.

Pre-Baby

I believe I was about 6 weeks pregnant when the horrid morning sickness kicked in. I was rarely sick though, more the feeling of nauseousness and wanting to be sick.

It was awful!

I remember trying random different things to help, like ginger biscuits (apparently ginger is good for morning sickness)! Unfortunately, this was not enough to prevent my frequent trips to the loo for a good heave!

I went off drinking tea! I was a massive fan of a brew at work so it was really strange that I just couldn't stomach one.

I was also ridiculously shattered all the time and wanted to sleep as soon as I got home from work. I'm sure Pete was thrilled by my exciting existence! Some days I barely made it to dinnertime before I was flat out on the sofa.

Once the first 12 weeks were over, and I had seen my scan with this tiny little person moving about, I knew all the feelings of yuck were well worth it! It was so surreal seeing my scan image on the screen, almost magical. I appreciate that as a species we would become extinct if we did not reproduce, and it is supposed to be **THE** most natural thing, but for me, it was something I really did not think would happen, even now, at the twelve-week mark!

I still had my off and tired days, but from twelve weeks onward I tried to enjoy things. In hindsight, if I could go back and talk to me, I would have stressed to enjoy the journey more! I worried so much and until I started showing, often questioned if it was real!

I remember feeling the baby kick for the first time (at about 19 weeks) and from then on, I knew I had this little character developing inside me.

My baby was called, 'Baby'… Very original, but it stuck (even to the point that when I had her, it took days to get used to her proper name!).

Pete and I had decided **NOT** to find out the sex, hence, 'Baby', seemed unisex and, well, obvious!

So yeah, I got fat!

One thing I did enjoy whilst being pregnant was being able to wear tight clothes that showed off my bump. It was ace! I've never been a lady for bodycon style dresses, but me with a baby bump felt pretty hot!

I remember my mum going shopping with me to buy some new clothes. We managed to find some nice maternity jeans and a dress. I was only about 14 weeks or so pregnant, but it was so exciting in the changing rooms looking at my little bump under my clothes. That was the first time the excitement really kicked in.

Summary Paragraph #2

I had a couple of little scares throughout the pregnancy with reduced movement, but these turned out to be fine. One thing I will advise to anyone with any worries during pregnancy is to ...

...trust your instincts ...

and never worry about getting yourself checked. I found I often questioned myself; was I having reduced movement or was I over-thinking? Whether it's one or twenty times, **never worry and just get checked!** The hospital was always lovely and reassured me every time that I was doing the right thing.

I have spoken to many mums since having my daughter, some of which loved being pregnant, and some who hated it. All I will say is try to enjoy it the best you can as it is over in a flash.

I have already forgotten the feeling of a baby kicking inside me, and I almost took it for granted at the time. It is a very special period and one I will cherish. That said, if you hated it, that's perfectly acceptable!

Pre-Birth Preparations

Throughout my pregnancy I did try to get booked in on antenatal classes but unfortunately the area where I live did not have any at the time. I felt bad about this as assumed going to a class with a birthing partner was the, 'done', thing, so I decided to buy a DVD instead! With the internet at my fingertips and good ole Amazon to hand, I had selected a well-reviewed DVD that was an antenatal class that you feel you are sitting in on (but just watching on TV).

I highly recommend this as another option if classes are not available, or if you would rather prepare in the privacy of your own home.

You would think as a female I would kind of know what happens during birth, and I guess on paper I did, but hearing someone talk about how you know when your labour has started, and how many various positions you can be in to push a baby out, was certainly eye-opening!

I felt like a complete amateur, almost like I didn't deserve to be having a baby!

Daft when I look back now, but that is how I felt. I think in my mind I thought I should feel a certain way, or already know certain things, and if I didn't, I must be doing something wrong (but I'll go into that more later as this general thought reared its ugly head at many a time).

I remember googling what I would need to have prepared for when the baby arrived, such as clothes; bedding; nappies; bottles; breast pumps; nipple cream (I did not even know nipple cream was a thing), and so many other things I cannot remember!

Part of me was so excited, the other part petrified!!! How on earth was I going to get all these things sorted – and what if I forget something!

Most of the chats I had with various people whilst pregnant, from friends to family (and sometimes complete strangers), were generally very positive. Excitement about the baby coming and lots of the same conversations about our preparation for the imminent arrival.

Sometimes I found these chats quite overwhelming and scary; everyone seemed to know so much and were all so keen to share their advice and guidance (whether I wanted it or not). Generally, it was ace, but sometimes it was all a little too much and left me feeling a little deflated, as though I had an obligation to sap up all this information otherwise, I would get it wrong and fail!

I was fortunate enough to have excited family members who wanted to help us which was super useful! We knew money would be tight and so we did not buy everything new, nor did we turn down anyone who wanted to help contribute.

I beat myself up for a little while that I was not getting a new pram system, or a new crib for next to the bed, but the crux of it was, we just could not afford it. Pete and I agreed it would be a better use of the money we had saved to assist me with being off work.

I did buy new mattresses for the pram and crib for next to the bed, plus a new car seat but that was it with the bigger items.

Summary Paragraph #3

NEVER feel bad about how little or how much you know. We are all human and have had so many different experiences in our lives up until now. Some of us have many siblings, and family members who have popped out a load of kids, whereas others have had little to no experience around babies and have never even considered what they may or may not need to know prior to having a child themselves. I did give myself some stick for how little I thought I knew, but looking back, what did it matter?

It didn't! Is the answer to that.

Take on board however much advice others offer you that you are comfortable with. Do not feel that you must be a magic sponge and remember it all. Most people just want to help so just see it as,

'optional guidance'.

Regarding second hand items, our little ones are only little for a short period of time and the hundreds of pounds you can spend on new things that are obsolete within a blink of an eye, could really be better used elsewhere. Buying second hand is nothing to worry about or be ashamed of. I wish I had of felt better about it than I did at the time. Not only was I saving money, my little one didn't have a clue anyway! I think some people feel they only need swish, up to date gadgets and gizmos because society has made them feel this is what they need to have.

Don't get me wrong, if you really want to get everything brand spanking new, and this aids the excitement you are feeling about having a baby, that's ace too!! No judgement should be placed either way. My aim here though is to reassure (or try to) those who feel the pressures of society and perhaps do not have the funding to get everything they need from new.

Do what feels right.

The Birth

So, time had been ticking away and I had gotten used to having this huge bump hanging off the front of me! I must say though, the third trimester was a tough one! It was approaching June, and 2017 gave us a ridiculously hot few weeks of summer, (well ridiculously hot for what we are used to in the UK!) So needless to say, I was very warm and very uncomfortable!

Not being able to fasten my sandals was annoying, **yet very funny!** Not being able to shave my legs properly when in the shower was also annoying (I did get around this by having a bath).

My due date came and went, but one thing I had remembered from my antenatal class DVD was that with first babies, this is very normal as our bodies have not done this before!

I was called in to hospital for a 'sweep'. All part of trying to help get things (labour) going! Even now I couldn't tell you exactly why we have them as I have actually forgotten!

(I have just searched it on the internet! It basically separates the membrane from the amniotic sac away from the cervix and should release some hormones to help start labour off)!

So, there you go!

It's not the best of experiences but it doesn't last long.

Throughout my pregnancy, so many people spoke about false labour contractions and how I would know my labour had started; about things like losing your, 'Mucus Plug'…. (I had no idea what this was at the time – again another internet search); and waters breaking to name a few.

NB: Your mucus plug is exactly that. A collection of mucus that forms in your cervical canal to prevent infection and germs etc getting to the baby. In late pregnancy (and as an indication labour is on its way), this plug will fall away.

There were so many areas of pregnancy that so many people do not seem to talk about, it was mind blowing! I appreciate some of the more, well, squeamish elements to pregnancy may not be as widely publicised, but still, I would have liked to have known more about this somehow!

For instance, I always thought that when your waters broke, they went with a big, 'whooooosh', like a water balloon popping inside you! Nope – that is more rare apparently, and in fact a little bit of a leak (so you feel like you've wet yourself) is more common.

That is what happened to me.

This is one of the reasons I have chosen to write this book, I wanted to recall my birthing experience regardless of whether it was deemed negative or positive to me at that time. I hope that this will provide some reassurance to others that if you have a bad time, its ok (well it doesn't feel ok at the time – but it will be), and if you have worries or doubts, that's alright and perfectly normal too!

So where was I, ah yes, the birth! So, my contractions started in the middle of the night! Slow and far apart at first …

If I remember rightly, my waters had broken (or started to leak) a little earlier that evening so I had to put a sanitary towel on! It was a lovely, sexy brick as I referred to it.

I downloaded an app on my phone to try and track the contractions. This proved to be useless as they were so sporadic it was impossible to see a pattern forming. I ended up waking Pete to say that I thought it was all starting and we called the hospital. They asked how far apart my contractions were, and when I explained there was no real regularity, they did not seem too concerned and told me to try and stick it out at home until things progressed further.

This was easier said than done!

I was pretty tired so thought I would try and sleep in between contractions. This didn't go too well but I must have had some mini naps as it was closer to morning when I next checked the time. I woke Pete again as found the pain too much and this was when we called the hospital again and they told me to go in.

I was scheduled to give birth in the Consultant-led unit as the baby had measured big on one of my last scans. I was disappointed in this at the time as had asked for a water-birth and was now told this would not be possible. By the time it came to the big day however, I had come to terms with it.

On arrival we were given a lovely birthing room/suite where my contractions seemed to have almost stopped! I felt a right plonker, but the mid-wife explained that adrenaline can often disguise and slow down the contractions.

I am not sure if any of you readers will have heard this phrase, but I heard it a few times during my pregnancy. People referring to, **'leaving their dignity at the door on the way into hospital'**. I always laughed at this but my goodness they were so right!

Within a few minutes of being in the birthing room, the midwife asked if she could check my sanitary towel (as it was in my notes that I was, well, leaking)! She gave it a good feel and confirmed that would have been my waters breaking (I had already worked this bit out, but it was nice to know I was right with my instincts)!

I was then told to get comfortable on the bed and they started setting up my access to gas and air. Again, my contractions hadn't really made an official appearance yet, but I knew I was in for the duration now!

We contacted my mum who we had agreed would be with myself and Pete for the birth. I think it was about 6-6.30am by this time so a nice early start for her!

When she rocked up, the pain had started again and so I was trying to give the gas and air a go. There is apparently an optimum time to get all the gas in, so that it helps to reduce the intensity of a contraction. I was absolutely crap at getting this timing so felt it was doing bugger all!

I do remember at one point feeling as high as a kite and on top of the world. It was so funny. I wasn't sure whether I needed a number two and so asked permission to use the toilet and apologised in advance if it was a poo. My mum and Pete thought it was highly amusing but, in my head, it was the polite thing to do.

I was checked to see how far along I was, and I recall them saying I was 6cm dilated. By this point I really couldn't fathom the gas and air and asked for more pain relief. The midwife explained that if I put a request in for it now, I may be able to get an epidural sorted before it was too late. I agreed to this straight away.

She also explained that although my front waters had broken, my back waters were still intact and so they needed to break them to help things along. If you're sat wondering how they do this,

wonder no more!

23

It literally looks like a big knitting needle that is, well inserted, and will gently break your waters.

Luckily it did not take long before the doctors arrived with all the equipment needed to administer the epidural. I remember sitting off the side of the bed leaning into Pete. They told me to be extra still as they inserted the needle. I thought I would be nervous when this happened but to be honest, I really didn't care. Anything at that time would have been better than the pain I was feeling with the contractions.

I wish I had of written down exactly how my contractions felt because the human body is so sneaky, and within a few hours of giving birth, I had forgotten! All I remember is what I was thinking at the time. I knew they hurt, so I made a mental log of it to remind myself! It is a feeling incomparable to any other feeling I have ever experienced (which I guess it would be as we don't have a baby every day)!

Once the epidural kicked in it all changed, well for a few hours at least. I cannot remember the time exactly that I had it, but I remember having chit-chats with the midwife and my mum buying us all a sandwich at lunch.

Every now and then, the midwife would pop in a catheter to drain my bladder as the epidural prevented me from knowing when I needed to urinate, plus, I wasn't able to walk to the loo.

It was quite a surreal feeling as I can remember being able to still move my legs, and I also remember being hooked up to a machine monitoring my contractions and seeing the needle going mad each time a contraction came but feeling no pain.

It was ace!

What I had also noticed, was that my contractions had stayed random the whole way through my labour. There was no set amount within a few minutes as I assumed there would be.

It got to later in the afternoon and as I hadn't been progressing as quickly as they would have liked, they got the doctor in, and he agreed for me to be put on a hormone drip containing oxytocin. This is supposed to speed things up! **It do not recall it doing that for me.**

I remember feeling like I was hooked up to this thing for what felt like hours. They then brought the doctor in again who did another check on me and said that I wasn't too far, and it wouldn't be long before I could start pushing. I believe I was between 9 and 10 centimetres dilated but he, er, assisted in pushing me to the 10 when he did his internal! I do recall the midwife telling me I was not dilating evenly though which meant nothing to me at the time!

The moment I was told to relax and start pushing, was the moment I knew something was not right. It was so odd! Because this was my first child, how on earth would I know whether what I was feeling was right or wrong? For a few contractions, I kept telling myself that I was being a coward and that all I was feeling was simply the normal birthing process. My mum and the midwife kept telling me to push when they could see a contraction building, and although I felt no pain as such, I was sure something wasn't right. It was like I was in pain but not in pain at the same time. I managed to get up onto all-fours and thinking to myself,

'DO NOT forget this feeling'.

It was like I was trapped! I knew the baby needed to come out, but everything felt stuck!

I turned over onto my back and the midwife was trying to encourage me to get ready to push again. This time I knew something wasn't right and so crossed my legs and said I was not pushing! I felt like a child having a tantrum! She was not too impressed by this! Funny when I look back, but certainly **NOT** funny at the time.

When she could see that I was not going to play ball, she got the doctor in again who did some checks and offered for me to be taken for an emergency C-Section. I remember feeling crap I was going down this route, but so relieved at the same time.

Having a natural birth was something I really wanted, and I could see this was slipping away. But knew I couldn't continue pushing.

Because I had the epidural, they were able to administer the drugs needed to fully numb me through the same entry point in my back. This meant that I could stay awake for the procedure which I was really chuffed about.

I honestly couldn't tell you how long it was between a decision being made to have the C-Section and the point at which I was in the operating theatre. Could have been minutes, could have been hours - **who knows!**

I remember saying bye to my mum who was in floods of tears. I think at this point she wasn't sure what was happening and whether I would be ok, but she could see that I knew something was not right. Pete was allowed into theatre and sat with me the whole time. He is a little on the squeamish side so chose to keep his eyes on my face and **NOT** where they cut me open and take the baby out!

To be fair, they do put up a little blue screen type thing to stop any dodgy viewing, but his eyes were fixated on my face none-the-less!

Again, I have no concept of time in my mind, but it was just after midnight, (I later found out 12:17am) when she made her first appearance!

They showed her to us, and I honestly thought it was a boy! Turns out her bits were swollen (completely normal), so I was corrected and told it was a girl!

Also, my gut instinct about something not being quite right was, well, **quite right!** It turns out, madam had twisted whilst I was trying to push and so she was in a position where I would have struggled to push her out without it causing me and her distress and making a mess out of me!

She was effectively stuck!

Baby DOB: **07.06.2017**

Weight: **3.95KG (8lb7oz) – YEP – not the smallest!**

Total labour time: **41h 47mins – says it all!**

Presentation at birth (baby position): **Cephalic occiput posterior** –

(cephalic = head down which is good, occiput posterior = a malposition – not ideal for a natural birth – some people know it as being born, 'star gazing', but basically it is being face up).

Summary Paragraph #4

On reflection, the type of birth you end up having can vary massively. Being prepared and knowing what you want is great (a birthing plan), but I also feel it is a case of coming to terms with the fact that no matter how well prepared you think you are, and how sure you are of the type of birth you are going to have, the baby will ultimately make the final decision.

I have had friends who wanted home births, friends who have used hypnotherapy (hypnobirthing), and all sorts of other weird and wonderful methods.

Some of them were able to have the exact type of birth they wanted, and others were the complete opposite. Having an agenda in mind is great, but also accepting that it may differ hugely from this is worth knowing too.

Some people seem to manage very well and have what seems like a beautiful birth, others scream with pain! I think I was somewhere in between. Having the pain relief was amazing and I am so glad I agreed to it. As my labour was so lengthy, I was exhausted enough as it was, let alone doing it with no additional medication.

I guess the crux of it is to again, **trust your instincts,** and do not feel you have let yourself down if you end up deviating from your original birthing plan. You can never anticipate what could go wrong, or how you will feel during a birth, so it's worth keeping your mind open to all possible eventualities.

Some mums want a C-Section from the get-go and are entitled to this. I personally do not see what it matters, and each individual should be happy and comfortable making the decision that suits them.

Some mums swear by all natural births, and many aim for a medication free or medication reduced birth.

In my opinion, if the baby is delivered safely, and both baby and mum are happy and healthy, that is a job well done!

The Baby - Feeding & Adapting

So, there she was, this little human had made her way into the world! Unfortunately, due to a reaction to the anaesthetic, I was very shaky and could not hold her straight away. She was given to Pete for a little while before I was ready. I don't really remember much of this – which is a pity as I'd have loved to have had those precious first moments (like you see on TV where they hand you the baby and you cry and hug) … **not with me!** I was stitched up and needed to calm before my little girl came anywhere near me.

When the time came for a hold, they tried to get her latched straight onto the boob for a feed. Again, I didn't really have much of an idea what was going on but knew that it was necessary so held her and went with the flow. I don't really remember much about how I felt (likely down to the medication), but it certainly wasn't an overwhelming feeling of love!

Just confusion and nothingness.

The birth and my initial time in the hospital was all a bit of a whirlwind. I was in for one night and out the following afternoon! Very quick considering I'd had a C-Section, but the staff were quick to try and get me up on my feet and walking, weeing, and pooing so I could go home.

I do recall some random moments whilst I was in the hospital that seem to have stuck….

Mini Moment 1.

Ok, so when I had finally become more lucid and aware of my surroundings, I remember looking across at the little clear plastic crib next to me and being petrified of the human lying in there, sound asleep. No negative feelings, but just mild panic setting in that it was up to me to keep this human alive. I remember the health care assistant coming in to check on us and asking if I had changed her nappy….' Er, no'… was my response. She looked at me, smiled and did it for me… I really was oblivious to the fact that perhaps I should have checked, but then, think about it - I had just gone through an emergency C-Section – a crappy reaction to medication, lack of sleep not to mention being a first-time mum… how was I supposed to know to check whether her nappy needed doing?!?

So yeah, I think the morale of that little recollection is do not feel bad if you really don't have a clue when you should be feeding, or when you should be changing nappies **– always ask and never be afraid to get extra help.**

Mini Moment 2

So, again on my first (and only) night in the hospital, I'd had a go at feeding, and was exhausted, I just could not keep my eyes open. One of the nurses popped in to see how we were and kindly offered to take the baby (still no official name yet), to the nurse's office while I slept. This was a complete gesture of good will and something I assume they commonly offer to do! My immediate response was,

'YES!' The prospect of having some sleep knowing that my baby would be watched over seemed like a no-brainer.

Well…. Less than ten minutes later I realised it was not possible for me to relax without her next to me, all sorts of scary thoughts came into my head…

Where was she?

Would they steal her?

Is she safe?

Has there been a zombie apocalypse and she's gone forever?…

So, I clambered out of bed very unsteadily and had to go and retrieve her. That was when I realised a connection had been made without me even realising. This little human being (as scary as she seemed) had become the most precious thing to me. Of course, she was perfectly fine and sound asleep, but I needed her back with me.

Ok so that's the end of my mini stories so I will carry on…

The following afternoon they let me home, but not before the baby was bathed! Weirdly I hadn't even thought about that either! She was still covered in all her, well, after birth stuff and I had no idea what her hair actually looked like as it was all stuck together!

The health care assistant set up a bath and while Pete was there, we bathed her together ready to go home. Boy did she cry! She did not enjoy that one bit (I still come across the pictures I took from time to time on my phone and smile).

So off we went home. It was the strangest feeling ever going home with this little baby, (we had agreed to name her Edie, but as mentioned at the start of this book, it took days for that to stick)!

I was exhausted and desperate for a shower, so Pete offered to keep an eye on Edie, who was sleeping, and I went and got cleaned up. I was in a lot of pain though with my stitches and dressing over my tum from the C-Section, it was horrid.

From the start of my pregnancy, I had made the decision that I wanted to try and breast feed. Some of this was a decision I made for myself, but some of it was also feeling that it was the right thing to do based on everyone else's opinions.

I must admit, it was the hardest thing I have ever done!

Edie seemed to have no problems latching on, but I felt like I was literally feeding her every few minutes. The first few nights were hell! Tiredness, constant feeding, fear in general of this tiny being! Seems daft looking back but it was so very real! I honestly felt I was out of my depths. Pete couldn't do much to help as I was exclusively breast feeding and it was just a very lonely period.

Day 4 after birth came along and it was my 31st birthday! I had a few family members round to wish me well, but I was not in a good place. Again, another common occurrence a few days or so after birth is your hormones adjusting themselves and settling down (baby blues). I felt so low and emotional. I didn't want to celebrate my birthday; I dreaded feeding Edie as it had now become painful as well as so flippin' often. This is where the miraculous nipple cream did come in handy although it didn't completely stop the cracking nipples that I was experiencing!!!

My mum wasn't far away though! Due to my C-Section, there was a lot I was not supposed to do such as heavy lifting and bending etc, so she assisted a lot with washing, cooking, cleaning – it was a real god send! Pete also had the first two weeks after the birth off, so I felt very well supported – just very low and miserable! Nobody seems to warn you about this prior to giving birth, it's one of those unspoken occurrences. I just wanted to stay in my Pjs and adjust in my own time, but I had heard so many stories of people being up and about soon after birth, so again I put pressure on myself to do more than I was ready to do.

One of my friends who had two girls of her own did send me lots of comforting text messages over the first few days to pre-warn me that I would have these low moments, that I would want to cry lots, that I would be so exhausted I wouldn't know how to get to the next day. I'm not sure she knows this, but I will forever be grateful for those little messages as it was the reassurance I needed. All these feelings I experienced were just never expected! Nobody ever seems to talk about these negative, crazy tired moments of despair (or at least if they had it wasn't with me!). Nobody prepares you for those first couple of weeks or so, but I can tell you now, it does get better, and when that light starts to shine, it all falls into place and you kind of adapt.

I think it's when you get to the point where you forget what life was like before the baby that you accept, adapt, and surrender to this new life.

Also, just to add in (so that you do not think it was all doom and gloom), every time I looked at Edie throughout these lower moments, I felt warm and fuzzy inside! I don't think I necessarily fell in love with her straight away, but I felt the need to do everything for her (willingly), regardless of how I was feeling. I knew that her experience coming into this World must have been scarier than mine.

Edie had her first midwife visit and had lost too much weight, so she advised I consider topping her up with some formula to supplement her. She assured me I could go back to exclusively breast feeding if I wanted to. **<u>I felt so crap about this;</u>** how could I not be giving her enough milk? Why had she lost too much weight? The feeling of failure came creeping in! I did take her advice though, and we got some formula in and tried to see how Edie would take to a bottle.

Fortunately, she was like a duck to water! She was happy to take boob or bottle, so I was able to go between the two. This allowed Pete to have more involvement with her feeding and give me some respite. I decided whilst she was feeding with Pete that I would try to express some milk ready for her next feed. This was advised to keep my milk flowing, but the problem was, I felt like an animal hooked up to a milking machine all day! I was either feeding Edie or trying to express. My body also did not like to part with milk artificially – I was lucky if I expressed 50ml! I felt rubbish about this too! Clearly it worked for some people, but just not me.

Over the next few weeks Edie gained weight well and I continued to combination feed her. For my own state of mind at the time, I decided I couldn't go back to exclusively breast feeding or expressing. I just couldn't face it. I felt awful, like a failure…. **again**, but I just couldn't do it.

I even felt pressured by a female doctor I spoke to about how, 'easy', it would be to get back to exclusively breastfeeding. She spoke to me like it was something I had to do. I felt too ashamed to tell her that it wasn't my plan to go back to this. Could she not see that really wasn't what I needed to hear. I already felt bad enough that I wasn't solely breastfeeding, that I couldn't express enough so Edie didn't have to have formula, and that I surrendered to the fact that this was how it needed to be for me.

I never really spoke to anyone in any depth about how rubbish I felt about this. I saw a breastfeeding specialist for advice and really tried to get my mind set around going back to exclusively breast feeding, but I just could not do it! The guilt played on my mind for months, perhaps years after having Edie but for my own state of mind, I had to stick to my guns.

Summary paragraph #5

As a first-time mum, with no idea how things will turn out down the line, you feel that every decision you make is critical to the wellbeing of your child. Little did I realise, all Edie wanted and needed was a mum who felt happy and comfortable in her own skin. I can see that now looking back, and my mum used to tell me the same at the time, so it wasn't that I wasn't helped or supported, it was how I felt inside me about how I was doing.

Feeling low; tired; overwhelmed; and generally shitty is normal for the first few days (maybe weeks) after giving birth. Our bodies are adjusting and what we have been through is **HUGE!** It's bad enough having to go through these naturally occurring emotions let alone putting more pressure on ourselves to do things a set way!

Do not put pressure on yourself to get dressed and looking marvellous within days after giving birth.

Do not worry about housework and whether things are a mess for visitors.

Do not worry about saying no to visitors if you just need time for yourself, they will understand.

Basically, do not feel there is a set way to go about anything! There isn't. Some people are naturally more energetic and may want to get up and sorted quite soon after having a baby (especially if they've had one prior to this). Some people enjoy wanting to keep their homes tidy and presentable for guests and their own frame of mind. None of this means you have to. You need to listen to yourself and do what feels right for **you**. These first few weeks/months will fly by and in no time at all you will look back, and how you dealt with them really won't matter.

Another thing not to feel bad about is the decision you make when feeding your baby. Of course, many say breast is best, but what is really best (in my opinion), is the wellbeing of the mum! They say babies' sense when you are tense and stressed and it can rub of onto them. All baby needs is food in their belly and a loving, relaxed environment. If breast is the way forward for you, that's ace! If it isn't, that's ace too!

Many of my friends who had babies within a few months of me, were able to successfully breast feed. They found it tough at first but managed to plough through and stick to it. It really worked for them, and what I had to keep telling myself is that it simply did not work for me, and that is ok!

I ended up thinking of the positives of my situation and about how it allowed Pete to share these bonding moments with Edie and provide me with some time to take five! I'm not saying one is better than the other, but I **am** saying you must go with what works for you and allows you to function.

Try not to feel bad if you do decide to bottle feed. It might be you don't want to even begin breast feeding and want to go straight to a bottle. Again, that is ok too!

Baby Groups

So, baby groups! I was never really sure of them, but they are something to try if you're looking to meet other new mums. I looked up various groups in my area whilst I was on maternity leave as felt it would be good to get out and about with Edie.

It's strange you know; when you are with a new baby, in your little maternity bubble, you kind of feel you have ventured into this whole other world of new mums and babies. Clearly, they have been there all along, but you never notice when you're living your day-to-day childless life.

I found a music class that took my fancy; a mixture of baby sensory but with instruments and singing. I have always loved music so this seemed like a great one to try. I think Edie was about 4 months old before I had plucked up the courage to attend a class though! The class was really nice, and everyone was very pleasant. Some of the mums went for a coffee and cake after the class which I was invited to. I did try a few times, but perhaps due to my own insecurities on feeding, I didn't really feel like I fit in. I let my worries about feeding and the decisions I had made with Edie spoil my opportunity to make friends with others.

Many of them were speaking about breast feeding and other facts of life, and I just felt completely disengaged from it all.

I still attended the music classes though! Edie and I went to them until the Covid lockdown in March 2020 and the more relaxed I became, the more I loosened up and enjoyed it too.

I didn't go to any other classes with Edie. I did feel bad about this, but I just didn't fancy it. Many of the mums had a different class each day of the week! **It just seemed like too much for me.**

Summary Paragraph #6

Baby groups are a good thing to have access to. If you want to meet other mums, and provide a change of scenery for your baby, they can be great. It is clear that babies benefit from stimulation and so having these classes can help them to engage more with the world around them. Don't forget to make sure you look at baby classes as something for you as a parent too; you need to take something positive from them.

If you do not feel that a baby group is for you, and you would rather not go to one, do not beat yourself up about this. I know people who never attended any at all and I know people who attended loads of them!

If you do go to a group and start chatting with other parents, it is a great opportunity to listen to various ways in which they all chose to go about their routines. If I hadn't of been so worried about bottle feeding Edie, I am sure I would have benefited from listening to their stories.

The Baby - Sleeping Routines

As you will recall I mentioned being quite a relaxed individual. Turns out this had also rubbed off on Edie. We enjoyed lazy mornings in bed (she used to have a morning breast feed), and we enjoyed not getting dressed straight away (well I did for sure). When I spoke to others about this, some were surprised that we were not up and about at the crack of dawn. I then began to question myself and whether I was doing something wrong. Should I be waking up at 6am with Edie and starting our day? Was getting up after 10 not the done thing? I think because of Edie's relaxed nature, I kind of went with the flow and kept things on a fluid, baby-led basis. If she was wide awake and not wanting to chill, of course I would get up, but if she was happy to feed and snooze then I'm going to cash in!!

Because it was so hot the first few weeks after having Edie, she didn't really wear much. Some nights it was just a nappy and I used to worry about the temperature being too high, or too low! My mum ended up telling me to think about how I felt, if I was too hot then Edie probably was too, and the same for feeling cold. This worked quite well.

Some of my friends swaddled their little ones and found this worked well for them. I felt I couldn't really do this with the heat but luckily Edie did not seem to mind.

Pete and I did not really have any set bedtime routine for Edie over the first few months. She slept when she wanted to sleep, fed when she wanted to feed, and stayed downstairs with us until we went to bed. She had her own Moses basket to snooze in, but a lot of the time she enjoyed lying on the sofa with us in sight where we could talk and gaggle to her and keep an eye on her once she had fallen asleep. She would then transfer into the crib next to the bed and continue to sleep. After about 6 weeks or so, she was pretty much sleeping through! We were so chuffed as had not really given the sleeping patterns much thought.

I know for sure this is different from baby to baby though! Some of my pals who had babies not long after me were keen to get into a routine as quickly as possible. This suited them and allowed them to function the way they wanted and needed to. They preferred to have set bedtime and nap routines and felt it benefitted their little one. For me personally, I just couldn't be too structured. I wasn't like that before having Edie, and providing she was perfectly fine with it, why would I be like that afterward? I felt for a long time that I was keeping a crazy secret about us not getting up early, and about Edie not having a set bedtime. I felt others would frown at me as though I was a bad parent, so I kept a lot of this between Pete and me.

Another common talking point between me and other parent pals was whether Edie was in her own room yet or not. Edie stayed in our bedroom with us until she was one. It worked for us to have her in there and she seemed to settle better. She grew out of the crib next to my bed fairly quickly and at about 5 months when she could sit up and move about more, we put her into a little cot at the bottom of our bed. Some of this was because we enjoyed having her with us, some of it was down to the fact we still hadn't fully finished decorating her room yet (DOH).

Some of my friends had their little ones in their own room at 3-4 months old. This worked for them and goes to show just how varied it can be from one household to the next.

Summary Paragraph #7

You may have picked up on a pattern with my summaries now but I'm going to say it again...

you have to do whatever suits you as a parent(s).

I have no idea whether I was in a minority or not with my more laid-back morning routine, but I certainly felt I was. Looking back now it really didn't matter and has had no adverse impact on myself or Edie. If anything, I am told how lucky I am that I had as much sleep as I did! One advantage of the way we chose to do things was that we were never held to ransom on when Edie was napping or needed to go to bed. It meant we could still go ahead with some of our plans, whether it was going to see a friend or popping out for a meal, Edie just came along. If she needed to sleep, she didn't mind where she slept and would still have a nap regardless of her location. I appreciate this won't suit everyone though and many prefer to ensure they are home and/or work their plans around nap time.

Every baby adapts to this new world they are living in at their own pace and in their own time. Perhaps if Edie had of been a lighter sleeper, or did not sleep as well, we would have considered introducing more structure to aid both her and us.

The Baby - Weaning

One thing I was fairly strict with was when I decided to try Edie on solid food. She seemed to cope well with her milk routines and never got upset for more, so I never rushed solids and started her at 6 months as advised. I was dreading the start of the weaning journey …

Do I go with baby-led?

Do I go with traditional?

I ended up settling on a book that was very colourful and full of more pictures than words! It helped me to focus on things without getting too overwhelmed. The book suggested starting babies with pureed vegetables before fruit so that they do not get too much of a sweet tooth.

This sounded logical to me so mashed potato it was!!

Some of the books I had were absolutely brilliant for advice on batch cooking your food and how you could store them to save time etc (for example I used a silicone ice tray to put my batches into as they were perfect baby sized portions that I could push out of the tray and heat up when needed).

Once I had a few tips in mind, I decided to go with my gut (excuse the pun)! I wanted Edie to eat healthily, and I wanted to know she had gotten a certain amount of nutrients from her food each day, so I went with traditional weaning with a twist of baby led. For instance, if she was having mashed potato and broccoli, I would also give her a soft piece of potato and small tree of broccoli to hold in her hand and try. This way she could mess with the food (including shoving it in her mouth and/or on the floor) as much as she wanted, but I was also able to feed her the food I had mashed and prepared.

This seemed to work really well and although it was messy, Edie really seemed to enjoy playing and feeling the food, as well as having it spoon fed into her mouth.

It wasn't long before I introduced pureed fruits and she gradually went from one meal a day, to two, and then to three.

Once Edie started eating solids, I stopped breast feeding. At this point I was only feeding morning and evening, so it felt like the right time to call it a day and Edie never really asked for it. Looking back, I am sad I did not do it for longer, but happy I gave it a go and managed to stick it out for as long as I did.

Summary Paragraph #8

I am sure you know what I am going to say now! Yep, that's right! When it comes to weaning, choose whichever method you feel will be best for your little one.

Some babies take a huge interest in their food and want to feed themselves; some take a huge interest in their food and DONT want to feed themselves; some are simply not interested in interacting with food and are happy to be fed, at least until they are a little older and more aware. Only you know your baby's personality and how you feel they will get on.

I chose a combination of both and that worked well for me.

You may even choose to swap and change; they could have a baby-led breakfast and a hearty pureed lunch followed by a mixture for dinner. It is a case of selecting a method and tweaking it as you go. Do not feel it is a failure if something doesn't go quite as you plan.

They all get to the same point in the end.

Life Now

I am writing this book 5 years after having Edie. She is currently at the start of her life at school and embarking on her own journey of learning and making friends.

She is fiercely independent, yet very loving. She still has a laid-back manner (as you would expect having us as parents), but we do try to enforce more routine with her.

Pete and I agreed that when the time came for nursery and school, her bedtimes would need to allow her to have as close to twelve hours sleep as possible. We knew that learning is something that can only be done with a wide-awake mind! Don't get me wrong, she will still try to stay up later, and when she is in bed, we cannot force her to go to sleep, but generally it works. She looks forward to a weekend when her brothers come to stay as she is allowed a later night to spend time with them.

She also enjoys cuddles in the morning and has been known to sneak into our bed in the night! Many will say that it is a bad habit to let them do this and they should be staying in their own bed, however I absolutely love and value these moments as I know they will not last forever. I know the time will come where she doesn't want cuddles in bed, and I know I will miss those times terribly. Perhaps it is selfish of me, but I love our snuggles and will cherish them for as long as Edie wants to have them.

One thing she isn't though is lazy! Although she enjoys her sleep and having late nights at weekends, when she is up and about, she has so much energy. She enjoys swimming and kickboxing and adores her friends.

Another thing I have noticed about this age, is the sheer number of clubs and activities that some of her peers do. Swimming, horse-riding, gymnastics, football, I could go on... all on a different day of the week. Chaos with parents rushing around from one activity to another.

Again, this may be what they thrive on, and if their little one's love all the clubs they are a part of then happy days! Edie does two activities; council led swimming lessons and kickboxing. If she wants to do more she can ask, and if we can afford it, we will gladly allow her. I guess it's what suits each family but having time after school to just play at home after dinner is something else Edie and I enjoy. These cherished moments of making memories doesn't cost anything and gives her a good balance of activities and time at home.

Sometimes I look back and wonder whether things would have worked differently if we had of been in more of a strict routine beforehand, but I guess we will never know. One thing I do know however, is that she is absolutely fine and loving life. Her lovely quirks and characteristics are a combination of her upbringing and own personality.

Whether she was purely breast fed or not - doesn't matter.

Whether she was put into her own room early on or stayed in with us for longer - doesn't matter.

Whether we were up at the crack of dawn or lazy bums - doesn't matter.

I could go on! But I think you get the gist!

What I do know looking back, is that I definitely worried too much about the decisions I made. I allowed guilt to play a part far too often and needed to cut myself some slack. Nobody is perfect and we will all make decisions we may later regret, or not get things right first time. In essence if you ensure you look after yourself and your wellbeing, then life with your little one will be so much more fun for you both.

I've also learned not to judge or have a negative opinion on how others choose to raise their children. Like I said right at the start of this book, we would all be rather boring if raised the same way! Our little mini humans need love, and most importantly our time. Don't get me wrong I am not perfect and modern life with all the gadgets, gizmos and social expectations can easily take over, but I guess that is a whole other story for another day - **or perhaps another book!**

In the meantime, enjoy your journey, whatever stage you are on, and look after yourself!

Summary Paragraph Family

As promised at the beginning of my book, here are my, 'Summary Paragraph's' consolidated for you to go through in one go.

Summary Paragraph #1

When you find out you are pregnant, it is ok and perfectly normal to feel a bit odd about everything, even completely out of your depths. I couldn't really nail the exact emotion I felt when I found out; maybe it was a lot of varying emotions rolled into one!

It's also ok to question whether you have done the right thing, and it is ok to feel amazing and excited too!

At one point I did wonder whether I had made the right choice but looking back I can see it was a period of adjustment for me and coming to terms with the journey I was about to embark upon.

Looking back, I think I was very lucky that I managed to get caught pregnant so quickly. I have friends who tried for months and months before they managed to conceive. Whether it takes a few weeks or a few months, it is normally not anything to worry about and will hopefully happen in good time and when your body is ready.

Always trust your body and your feelings though, and if you have any concerns about conceiving do not hesitate to speak to a doctor about things.

Summary Paragraph #2

I had a couple of little scares throughout the pregnancy with reduced movement, but these turned out to be fine. One thing I will advise to anyone with any worries during pregnancy is to ...

...trust your instincts ...

and never worry about getting yourself checked. I found I often questioned myself; was I having reduced movement or was I over-thinking? Whether it's one or twenty times, never worry and just get checked! The hospital was always lovely and reassured me every time that I was doing the right thing.

I have spoken to many mums since having my daughter, some of which loved being pregnant, and some who hated it. All I will say is try to enjoy it the best you can as it is over in a flash.

I have already forgotten the feeling of a baby kicking inside me, and I almost took it for granted at the time. It is a very special period and one I will cherish. That said, if you hated it, that's perfectly acceptable!

Summary Paragraph #3

NEVER feel bad about how little or how much you know. We are all human and have had so many different experiences in our lives up until now. Some of us have many siblings, and family members who have popped out a load of kids, whereas others have had little to no experience around babies and have never even considered what they may or may not need to know prior to having a child themselves. I did give myself some stick for how little I thought I knew, but looking back, what did it matter?

It didn't! Is the answer to that.

Take on board however much advice others offer you that you are comfortable with. Do not feel that you must be a magic sponge and remember it all. Most people just want to help so just see it as,

'optional guidance'.

Regarding second hand items, our little ones are only little for a short period of time and the hundreds of pounds you can spend on new things that are obsolete within a blink of an eye, could really be better used elsewhere. Buying second hand is nothing to worry about or be ashamed of. I wish I had of felt better about it than I did at the time. Not only was I saving money, my little one didn't have a clue anyway! I think some people feel they only need swish, up to date gadgets and gizmos because society has made them feel this is what they need to have.

Don't get me wrong, if you really want to get everything brand spanking new, and this aids the excitement you are feeling about having a baby, that's ace too!! No judgement should be placed either way. My aim here though is to reassure (or try to) those who feel the pressures of society and perhaps do not have the funding to get everything they need from new.

Do what feels right.

Summary Paragraph #4

On reflection, the type of birth you end up having can vary massively. Being prepared and knowing what you want is great (a birthing plan), but I also feel it is a case of coming to terms with the fact that no matter how well prepared you think you are, and how sure you are of the type of birth you are going to have, the baby will ultimately make the final decision.

I have had friends who wanted home births, friends who have used hypnotherapy (hypnobirthing), and all sorts of other weird and wonderful methods. Some of them were able to have the exact type of birth they wanted, and others were the complete opposite. Having an agenda in mind is great, but also accepting that it may differ hugely from this is worth knowing too.

Some people seem to manage very well and have what seems like a beautiful birth, others scream with pain! I think I was somewhere in between. Having the pain relief was amazing and I am so glad I agreed to it. As my labour was so lengthy, I was exhausted enough as it was, let alone doing it with no additional medication.

I guess the crux of it is to again, **trust your instincts**, and do not feel you have let yourself down if you end up deviating from your original birthing plan. You can never anticipate what could go wrong, or how you will feel during a birth, so it's worth keeping your mind open to all possible eventualities.

Some mums want a C-Section from the get-go and are entitled to this. I personally do not see what it matters, and each individual should be happy and comfortable making the decision that suits them.

Some mums swear by all natural births, and many aim for a medication free or medication reduced birth.

In my opinion, if the baby is delivered safely, and both baby and mum are happy and healthy, that is a job well done!

Summary Paragraph #5

As a first-time mum, with no idea how things will turn out down the line, you feel that every decision you make is critical to the wellbeing of your child. Little did I realise, all Edie wanted and needed was a mum who felt happy and comfortable in her own skin. I can see that now looking back, and my mum used to tell me the same at the time, so it wasn't that I wasn't helped or supported, it was how I felt inside me about how I was doing.

Feeling low; tired; overwhelmed; and generally shitty is normal for the first few days (maybe weeks) after giving birth. Our bodies are adjusting and what we have been through is HUGE! It's bad enough having to go through these naturally occurring emotions let alone putting more pressure on ourselves to do things a set way!

Do not put pressure on yourself to get dressed and looking marvellous within days after giving birth.

Do not worry about housework and whether things are a mess for visitors.

Do not worry about saying no to visitors if you just need time for yourself, they will understand.

Basically, do not feel there is a set way to go about anything! There isn't. Some people are naturally more energetic and may want to get up and sorted quite soon after having a baby (especially if they've had one prior to this). Some people enjoy wanting to keep their homes tidy and presentable for guests and their own frame of mind. None of this means you have to. You need to listen to yourself and do what feels right for you. These first few weeks/months will fly by and in no time at all you will look back, and how you dealt with them really won't matter.

Another thing not to feel bad about is the decision you make when feeding your baby. Of course, many say breast is best, but what is really best (in my opinion), is the wellbeing of the mum! They say babies' sense when you are tense and stressed and it can rub of onto them. All baby needs is food in their belly and a loving, relaxed environment. If breast is the way forward for you, that's ace! If it isn't, that's ace too!

Many of my friends who had babies within a few months of me, were able to successfully breast feed. They found it tough at first but managed to plough through and stick to it. It really worked for them, and what I had to keep telling myself is that it simply did not work for me, and that is ok!

I ended up thinking of the positives of my situation and about how it allowed Pete to share these bonding moments with Edie and provide me with some time to take five! I'm not saying one is better than the other, but I _am_ saying you must go with what works for you and allows you to function.

Try not to feel bad if you do decide to bottle feed. It might be you don't want to even begin breast feeding and want to go straight to a bottle. Again, that is ok too!

Summary Paragraph #6

Baby groups are a good thing to have access to. If you want to meet other mums, and provide a change of scenery for your baby, they can be great. It is clear that babies benefit from stimulation and so having these classes can help them to engage more with the world around them. Don't forget to make sure you look at baby classes as something for you as a parent too; you need to take something positive from them.

If you do not feel that a baby group is for you, and you would rather not go to one, do not beat yourself up about this. I know people who never attended any at all and I know people who attended loads of them!

If you do go to a group and start chatting with other parents, it is a great opportunity to listen to various ways in which they all chose to go about their routines. If I hadn't of been so worried about bottle feeding Edie, I am sure I would have benefited from listening to their stories.

Summary Paragraph #7

You may have picked up on a pattern with my summaries now but I'm going to say it again...

you have to do whatever suits you as a parent(s).

I have no idea whether I was in a minority or not with my more laid-back morning routine, but I certainly felt I was. Looking back now it really didn't matter and has had no adverse impact on myself or Edie. If anything, I am told how lucky I am that I had as much sleep as I did! One advantage of the way we chose to do things was that we were never held to ransom on when Edie was napping or needed to go to bed. It meant we could still go ahead with some of our plans, whether it was going to see a friend or popping out for a meal, Edie just came along. If she needed to sleep, she didn't mind where she slept and would still have a nap regardless of her location. I appreciate this won't suit everyone though and many prefer to ensure they are home and/or work their plans around nap time.

Every baby adapts to this new world they are living in at their own pace and in their own time. Perhaps if Edie had of been a lighter sleeper, or did not sleep as well, we would have considered introducing more structure to aid both her and us.

.

Summary Paragraph #8

I am sure you know what I am going to say now! Yep, that's right! When it comes to weaning, choose whichever method you feel will be best for your little one.

Some babies take a huge interest in their food and want to feed themselves; some take a huge interest in their food and DONT want to feed themselves; some are simply not interested in interacting with food and are happy to be fed, at least until they are a little older and more aware. Only you know your baby's personality and how you feel they will get on.

I chose a combination of both and that worked well for me.
You may even choose to swap and change; they could have a baby-led breakfast and a hearty pureed lunch followed by a mixture for dinner. It is a case of selecting a method and tweaking it as you go. Do not feel it is a failure if something doesn't go quite as you plan.

They all get to the same point in the end.

So there you have it. The journey from Me to Mum.

I hope it has been an enjoyable read for you but more importantly, I hope it provides some help and reassurance.

We are all human.

If you have enjoyed this book and want to create your own notes/thoughts of your journey, please check out my, **'From You to Mum - YOUR Journey'**, notebook.

In here you can write down anything you feel might be nice to look back on, or any important dates/activities that you embark upon on your journey.

Use it however you see fit!

Printed in Great Britain
by Amazon